BUG BOOKS

Stick Insect

Karen Hartley, Chris Macro and Philip Taylor

Heinemann Library
Chicago, IL

© 2003, 2008 Heinemann Library
an imprint of Capstone Global Library,LLC
Chicago, Illinois

Customer Service 888-454-2279
Visit our website at www.heinemannlibrary.com

All rights reserved. No part of this publication may be reproduced or transmitted in any form or by any means, electronic or mechanical, including photocopying, recording, taping, or any information storage and retrieval system, without permission in writing from the publisher.

Design: Kimberly R. Miracle and Cavedweller Studio
Illustration: Alan Fraser at Pennant Illustration

Originated by Dot Gradations Ltd
Printed and bound in China by South China Printing Company

12 11
10 9 8 7 6 5 4 3 2

New edition ISBNs: 978 1 4329 1235 2 (hardcover)
                    978 1 4329 1246 8 (paperback)

The Library of Congress has cataloged the first edition as follows:
    Hartley, Karen, Macro, Chris, and Taylor, Philip
    Stick insect. - (Bug books) / Hartley, Karen, Macro, Chris, and Taylor, Philip
        p. cm. -- (Bug books)
    Summary: Describes the physical characteristics, habits, and natural
    environment of the stick insect.
    Includes bibliographical references (p.   ).
     ISBN 978-1-4329-1235-2 (hardcover) -- ISBN 978-1-4329-1246-8 (pbk.)
     1.   --Juvenile literature. [1.   .] I. Title:
    II. Title. III. Series.

Acknowledgments
The publishers would like to thank the following for permission to reproduce photographs:
© Ardea pp. 7 (P. Goetgheluck), 16 (M. Iijima), 19 (P. Goetgheluck), 23 (P. Morris), 24 (A. Warren), 26 (A. Warren); © Bruce Coleman pp. 6 (L. Marigo), 9 (M. Fogden), 17 (A. Purcell), 20 (A. Purcell), 22 (A. Purcell); © NHPA pp. 10 (A. Bannister), 11 (A. Bannister), 18 (D. Heuclin); © Okapia pp. 8 (K. Sandved), 27 (B. Roth); © Oxford Scientific Films pp. 4 (M. Leach), 5 (J. Cooke), 13 (D. Fox), 14 (M. Leach), 29 (Mantis Wildlife Films); © Photolibrary (David Ennis) p. 25; © Science Photo Library pp. 12 (Dr Morley Read), 15 (Tony Camacho); © Small Life Supplies p. 21; © Trevor Clifford p. 28.

Cover photograph of a New Zealand stick insect reproduced with permission of FLPA (Geoff Moon).

Every effort has been made to contact copyright holders of any material reproduced in this book.
Any omissions will be rectified in subsequent printings if notice is given to the publisher.

Contents

Some words are shown in bold, **like this**. You can find out what they mean by looking in the glossary.

What Are Stick Insects?

Stick **insects** are very unusual insects. There are many types of stick insects but they all have a similar shape.

All stick insects have very long bodies.
Some types of stick insect have wings.

What Do Stick Insects Look Like?

leg

head

Some stick **insects** look like thin sticks.
They have six legs and a small head.
Most stick insects are green or brown.

Stick insects have a mouth and two big eyes. They can see up, down, backwards, and forwards at the same time. They have two **antennae** for feeling and smelling.

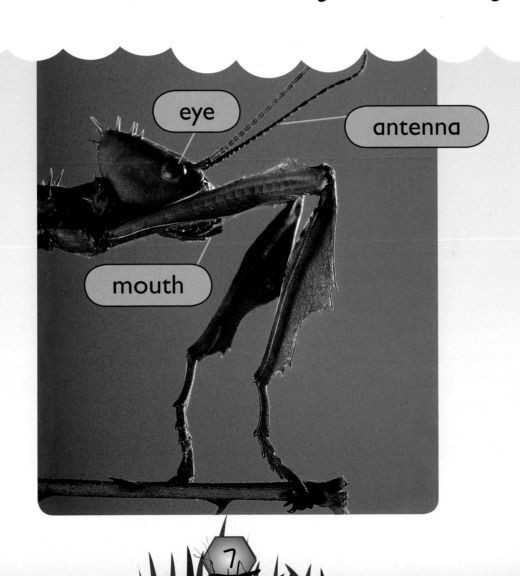

eye

antenna

mouth

How Big Are Stick Insects?

Most **adult** stick **insects** are about as long as your hand.

Some stick insects that live in **tropical countries** are bigger. They can be nearly as long as a ruler.

How Are Stick Insects Born?

egg

Female stick **insects** lay hundreds of eggs. Some eggs are hard and round, like little seeds. The baby stick insects can stay inside the eggs for a long time.

The babies that **hatch** out of the eggs are called **nymphs**. They look like tiny **adult** stick insects but they have no wings. Most baby stick insects are females. **Males** are very rare.

How Do Stick Insects Grow?

The **nymphs** grow quickly. They get too big for their skin. The old skin falls off and there is a new skin underneath. This is called **molting**.

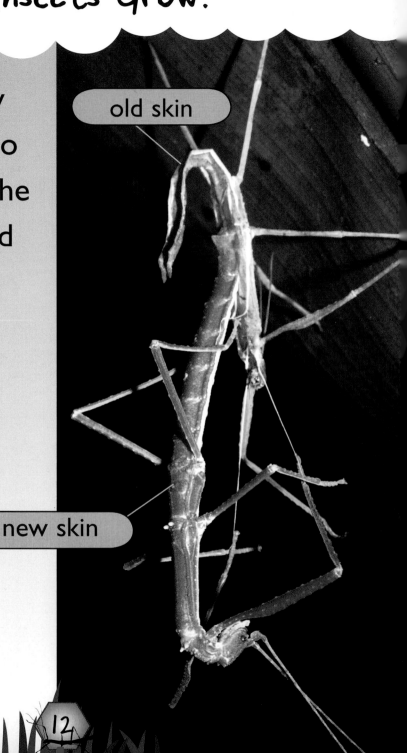

old skin

new skin

The new skin is very soft but it soon gets hard when it dries out. Some stick **insects** molt five or six times before they are **adults**.

How Do Stick Insects Move?

Stick **insects** walk slowly. They sway from side to side like a twig in the wind. When they are still, they point their two front legs out in front of them.

Some stick insects have a pair of wings. They can fly a short way. Sometimes they flash their wings to frighten **predators**.

wing

What Do Stick Insects Eat?

All stick **insects** eat leaves. They also drink water. Some stick insects look like the leaves they eat.

In Australia, there are lots of stick insects like the one in the picture. When they are hungry, they can eat all the leaves on a **eucalyptus tree**.

17

Which Animals Eat Stick Insects?

Lizards and birds eat stick **insects**.
In some hot countries, people eat
stick insects.

18

If a stick insect is in danger it stays very still. It looks just like a twig. This **camouflage** works so well that sometimes **predators** do not see it hiding.

Where Do Stick Insects Live?

Stick **insects** live in hot countries. They live where there are lots of trees and bushes so they can eat the leaves and hide from **predators**.

Some people keep stick insects as pets. They keep them warm. They keep them in tall cases so that the stick insects have room to climb.

How Long Do Stick Insects Live?

Lots of stick **insects** are eaten when they are still **nymphs**. **Adult** stick insects like this one can live for about a year.

Some adult stick insects live for nearly two years. They need food, shelter, and water to live.

What Do Stick Insects Do?

Stick **insects** can stay still for a long time. They hold on with special pads and claws on their feet.

Sometimes, if a stick insect is in danger, it will fall off a twig and lie on the ground pretending to be dead.

How Are Stick Insects Special?

If a young stick **insect** gets its leg trapped, it can escape by breaking it off. It will hobble around on five legs until a new one grows when it **molts**.

Stick insects have tiny holes called **spiracles** along their bodies. They breathe through these holes.

spiracle

Thinking About Stick Insects

This girl wants to keep a stick **insect** as a pet. What will the stick insect need to stay healthy?

In this photo, some stick insects are hiding. How many can you see? How are they **camouflaged**?

Bug Map

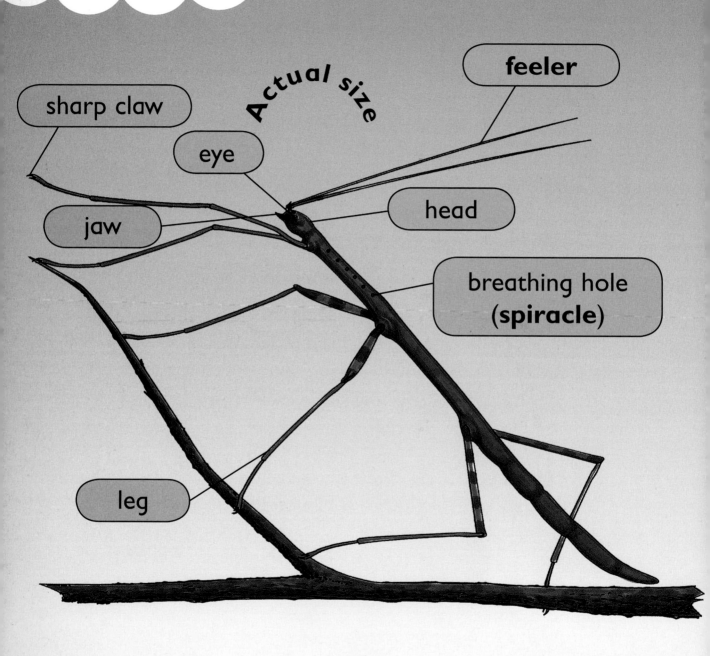

feeler

sharp claw

Actual size

eye

head

jaw

breathing hole (**spiracle**)

leg

Glossary

adult grown-up

antenna (more than one = antennae) thin tube that sticks out from the head of an insect. Antennae can be used to smell, feel, hear, or sense direction.

camouflage when an animal's color or shape helps it to hide

eucalyptus tree tree that is common in Australia

female animal that can lay eggs or give birth to live young. Women are females.

hatch break out of an egg

insect small animal with six legs and a body with three parts

male animal that can mate with a female to produce young. Men are males.

molting time in an insect's life when it gets too big for its skin. The old skin drops off and a new skin is underneath.

nymph insect baby that has hatched from an egg. It has no wings.

predator animal that hunts and eats other animals

spiracle breathing holes along a stick insect's body

tropical countries countries where it is very hot and there is a lot of rain

Index

More Books to Read

Kelly, Diane. *Bugs: Stick Insect.* Farmington Hills, MI: KidHaven Press, 2004.

Phillips, Dee. *My First Book of Bugs and Spiders.* Tunbridge Wells, UK: Ticktock Media, 2005.

Ross, Stewart and Jim Pipe. *Minibeasts: Going on a Bug Hunt.* London: Franklin Watts, 2006.